The
LITTLE BOOK OF
CULTS

T0349799

THE LITTLE BOOK OF CULTS

Text by Lucy York

An Hachette UK Company
www.hachette.co.uk

Summersdale Publishers
Part of Octopus Publishing Group Limited
Carmelite House
50 Victoria Embankment
LONDON
EC4Y 0DZ
UK

www.summersdale.com

Printed and bound in Poland

ISBN: 978-1-83799-358-1

This FSC® label means that materials used for the product have been responsibly sourced

MIX
Paper | Supporting responsible forestry
FSC® C018236

Substantial discounts on bulk quantities of Summersdale books are available to corporations, professional associations and other organizations. For details contact general enquiries: telephone: +44 (0) 1243 771107 or email: enquiries@summersdale.com.

The —
LITTLE BOOK OF
CULTS

Jamie King

summersdale

DISCLAIMER

The author and the publisher make no claim that the beliefs of any of these cults have any basis in fact. The beliefs and activities of these cults are included herein for entertainment purposes only. Every effort has been made to ensure that all information is correct. Should there be any errors, we apologize and shall be pleased to make the appropriate amendments in any future editions.

Contents

Introduction

When you hear or read the word "cult", what springs to mind? Brainwashing and orgies, perhaps? Peculiar rituals and outlandish beliefs? Maybe a bit of doomsday prepping and group suicide? You will find all of this and more in this petite introduction to the curious and often terrifying world of cults. The *Oxford English Dictionary* defines the word "cult" as:

> *"A relatively small group of people having (esp. religious) beliefs or practices regarded by others as strange or sinister, or as exercising excessive control over members."*

In the following pages you will read about some of the strangest and most sinister organizations ever to have existed, from the infamous Peoples Temple that culminated in the Jonestown massacre of 1978 to the lesser-known Church of the Most High Goddess that "spiritually cleansed" over 2,000 people in bizarre sex rituals in the 1980s. The cults discussed here have been divided up into religious, doomsday and sex cults, but as you will discover, many of them incorporated elements of all three. For each cult you will find out how it all began, what the followers believed, what life in the cult was like and how it all came to a – sometimes deadly – end.

RELIGIOUS CULTS

Defined by their distinctive dogmas and memorable for their charismatic leaders, the cults in this chapter have captured public attention through their unusual practices and sometimes tragic outcomes. Characterized by mind control, an insular worldview and an intense devotion to a central figure, these cults underscore the dark potential within the human search for spiritual meaning. Many of these cults found a basis in well-known existing world religions, but let's remember that these are fringe groups and they do not particularly represent the religions from which they sprang. Many of them cherry-picked doctrines from various faiths and combined them to form their own bizarre belief systems. To some it might seem that their leaders were… well, making it all up as they went along. But to the followers of these religious cults, their leaders' words were everything.

Peoples Temple

DATES ACTIVE:
1954–1978

FOUNDERS:
Jim Jones

LOCATION:
Indianapolis and California (US), Guyana

MEMBERS:
3,000–5,000

How it began

The Peoples Temple was founded by Jim Jones (1931–1978) in Indianapolis in 1954. The group became known for Jones's "faith healings", during which "cancerous tissues" (chicken livers and other animal parts that had been planted on those being "healed") were removed. In 1965, Jones moved the group to California, with headquarters in San Francisco and later a commune-like settlement in Redwood Valley. Jones became increasingly controlling of his followers, many of whom gave all their income and property to the Peoples Temple. Reports of abuse emerged, and the organization received a lot of negative publicity. In 1974, Jones ordered the construction of a new commune in Guyana, where he said the community would be safe from the global nuclear war he claimed was imminent and could live in a socialist paradise free from the oppressive US government. It was there that the most infamous cult mass suicide of all time would take place four years later.

What did they believe?

Affiliated with the Christian Church (Disciples of Christ), a Protestant Christian denomination, the Peoples Temple fostered some elements of Christianity and claimed to promote socialism and equality. It initially presented itself as a progressive and inclusive religious community with a focus on social justice. Jones advocated for racial integration, economic equality and communal living. But what really held the group together was Jones's charismatic leadership. He wielded significant control over his followers, promoting an ideology of utopian socialism while portraying himself as a messianic figure. Over time, the group's principles became increasingly authoritarian, culminating in the tragic events in Jonestown, which serve as a stark reminder of the dangers inherent in charismatic leadership and the manipulation of sincere beliefs for nefarious purposes.

The Gang of Eight

Once you were in the Peoples Temple, it wasn't all that easy to leave. In 1973, eight young members – known as the "Gang of Eight" – decided to flee together. But Jim Jones wasn't about to let them slip away unceremoniously into the night. He sent out multiple search parties, one of which surveyed the highways from a rented plane. The Gang of Eight headed for Canada. However, since they had a large number of firearms with them, which they feared trying to smuggle over the US-Canada border, they instead escaped into the hills of Montana. Following this mass defection, Jim Jones summoned 30 members to his home and announced that, "in order to keep our apostolic socialism, we should all kill ourselves and leave a note saying that because of harassment, a socialist group cannot exist at this time." Though the proposed suicides did not go ahead, it was a harbinger of the destruction to come.

How it ended

After the move to Guyana in 1974, the group lived for several years as the Peoples Temple Agricultural Project. By 1978, former members had begun speaking out against the organization, including alleging human rights abuses. It was rumoured that some of the people at Jonestown were being held against their will. In November of that year, San Francisco Congressman Leo Ryan travelled to the Jonestown settlement in Guyana to investigate. Ryan and several others of his delegation were fired on by members of the community and died. But the needless death didn't stop there. On 18 November 1978, Jim Jones ordered his congregation to drink a deadly mix of cyanide and Flavor Aid (not, as is commonly believed, Kool Aid), resulting in a mass suicide that claimed the lives of over 900 people. Until the 9/11 terrorist attacks, the incident held the record for the largest loss of American civilian life in history.

Jim Jones

Jim Jones was born on 13 May 1931 in Crete, Indiana. He was frequently neglected by his parents and neighbours described him as an unusual child obsessed with religion and death. At a young age he grew interested in Pentecostalism and had ambitions of becoming a preacher. In the 1950s, he was ordained as a Christian minister in the Independent Assemblies of God. He participated in the Pentecostal Latter Rain movement and the Healing Revival, and in 1954 he founded the organization that would become the Peoples Temple. He was a charismatic figure, known for his oratory skills and ability to captivate and inspire people. He presented himself as a passionate advocate for social justice and equality. However, beneath this façade, Jones exhibited traits of narcissism, paranoia and authoritarianism. As a leader, he wielded considerable control over his followers, employing manipulative tactics and psychological coercion.

Heaven's Gate

DATES ACTIVE:

1974–1997

FOUNDERS:

Marshall Applewhite and Bonnie Nettles

LOCATION:

New Mexico and California (US)

MEMBERS:

39

How it began

Founders Marshall Applewhite (1932–1997) and Bonnie Nettles (1927–1985) first met in 1972 at a hospital where Nettles worked as a nurse. The pair shared an interest in mysticism, religion and extraterrestrials. They concluded that they were the "two witnesses" described in the Book of Revelation – and that one day they would ascend to a higher level of existence on a spaceship. For this reason, they named themselves the "Heaven's Gate" group. In 1975, the pair held gatherings in California and Oregon, attracting their first followers. Around 20 people joined the group at this time, giving up their jobs and possessions and disappearing from society. The group travelled around the country, camping out and staying under the radar of authorities. In the early 1990s, they began to recruit more members, eventually heading to California, where they would settle in 1996.

Life in the cult

The close-knit group was only open to adults aged over 18. Everything was communally shared and members had to give up all possessions and cut off all contact with family and friends. In the years when Heaven's Gate was on the move, they lived a nomadic life of begging and destitution. They adhered to a rigid and ascetic set of behavioural rules. They had to "purify" their bodies of things like fast food and drugs using the Master Cleanse technique, invented in the 1940s by Stanley Burroughs. But Heaven's Gate took this to the extreme of drinking nothing but a mix of lemonade, cayenne pepper and maple syrup for three months. Sexual abstinence was also expected, and members were encouraged to adopt an asexual appearance. Applewhite and seven other male members even went so far as to voluntarily undergo castration.

What did they believe?

Heaven's Gate brought together elements of New Age belief, Christian millenarianism and ufology. Its core belief was that members of the group would be able to transform into immortal extraterrestrial beings by giving up their human nature. They would then ascend to the "Next Level" or "The Evolutionary Level Above Human" aboard a UFO. But in 1985, Nettles died from cancer, throwing this belief into doubt. Membership dwindled and the cult wasn't to resurface until the early 1990s. By then, members had come to think that the body was merely a "container" for the soul, which would be transferred to new "Next Level bodies" once they died. According to Applewhite, their chance was coming soon: in 1997, the Hale-Bopp comet was due to pass close to Earth, and hidden in its wake, he claimed, travelled the spaceship they had long awaited to carry them to the next level of existence.

How it ended

As the Hale-Bopp comet approached Earth, Applewhite began to make preparations. In 1996, he rented a large property near San Diego and moved in with the other remaining 38 members of the group. In late March 1997, the Hale-Bopp comet came within its closest distance to Earth. The Heaven's Gate crew were ready. Each member recorded a farewell message. Dressed in identical outfits (black sweatshirts and sweatpants and Nike Decades shoes) and with a five-dollar bill and three quarters tucked in their pockets, Applewhite and the members swallowed a deadly mix of phenobarbital and apple sauce. The bodies were discovered on 26 March after police received an anonymous tip. Whether or not the deceased members made it to the spaceship is unknown. As of the time of writing, the heavensgate.com website is still operational and run by a couple of the surviving original members.

Marshall Applewhite

Born in Texas on 17 May 1931, Marshall Applewhite was the son of a Presbyterian minister and was very religious even as a child. As a young man he attended several universities, served in the United States Army and went on to pursue a career in education until 1970, when he resigned from the University of St. Thomas in Houston, Texas, due to "emotional turmoil". His father died a year later, plunging him into a severe depression. In 1972, he met fellow cult founder Bonnie Nettles. With their shared interest in theosophy and biblical prophecy, the pair quickly became close. In August 1974, Applewhite was arrested for failing to return a rental car and was jailed for six months. He claimed that he kept the car because he had been "divinely authorized". It was when he got out that he and Nettles decided to contact extraterrestrials and began seeking followers.

Branch Davidians

DATES ACTIVE:
1955–present

FOUNDERS:
Benjamin Roden

LOCATION:
Waco, Texas (US)

MEMBERS:
100+
(around the time of the Waco Siege)

How it began

The Branch Davidians originated as a splinter group from the Davidian movement, which itself was an offshoot of the Seventh-day Adventist Church. The Davidians were founded in the 1930s by Victor Houteff, who claimed to be a prophet and called for reform in Seventh-day Adventist doctrine. After Houteff's death in 1955, leadership of the Davidians passed to his wife, Florence Houteff. However, internal divisions emerged, and one of the factions, led by Benjamin Roden, became known as the Branch Davidians. The Branch Davidians gained more prominence under the leadership of David Koresh (born Vernon Wayne Howell) in the 1980s. Under his leadership, the group shifted away from some traditional Davidian beliefs and developed its own theology. The most notorious incident involving the Branch Davidians was the siege of their communal residence of Mount Carmel in Waco, Texas, in 1993.

What did they believe?

The beliefs of the Branch Davidians evolved over time, and there were variations under different leaders. Under the leadership of David Koresh in the 1980s and early 1990s, the group predicted the imminent arrival of a catastrophic event that would precede the Second Coming of Christ. Koresh called himself the final prophet and the Lamb of God mentioned in the Bible. He claimed to have unlocked a special understanding of the prophecies in the Book of Revelation, and in particular, the seven seals mentioned in that book. He preached that his followers must accept his teachings to find salvation. In 1989, he announced that God had told him to procreate with the women in the group to create a "House of David" of his "special people". Married couples would be separated, and only he could have intercourse with the wives.

How it ended

In February 1993, the *Waco Tribune Herald* published a series of articles in which former cultists made allegations of child abuse and statutory rape against Koresh. The Davidians were also suspected of stockpiling illegal weapons. The Bureau of Alcohol, Tobacco, Firearms and Explosives (ATF) attempted to execute a search warrant. In the ensuing raid, four ATF agents and six Branch Davidians were killed. After the failed raid was a 51-day standoff. Negotiations took place between the FBI and Koresh, but these efforts to resolve the situation peacefully failed. On 19 April, the FBI launched a tear gas assault on the compound in an attempt to force the Branch Davidians to surrender. A few hours later, a fire broke out within the compound, consuming the Mount Carmel Center and resulting in the deaths of 76 people, including David Koresh. There are several groups that claim descent from the Branch Davidians in existence today, some of whom still believe the end of days is imminent.

David Koresh

David Koresh was born Vernon Wayne Howell on 17 August 1959 in Houston, Texas. Raised by a single mother, he had a tumultuous early life marked by poverty. He changed schools frequently and struggled with dyslexia, which affected his academic performance. In his late teens, he joined the Seventh-day Adventist Church, where he first encountered the Branch Davidians. Koresh was captivated by their teachings, particularly those of their leader, Lois Roden. After Lois Roden's death in 1986, Koresh was engaged in a power struggle against Benjamin Roden's son George, eventually emerging as the leader of the Branch Davidians. He and his followers took over Mount Carmel in 1987. Koresh was said to be both enigmatic and charismatic, capable of forging deep emotional connections with his followers. However, as his leadership of the Branch Davidians progressed, he became increasingly autocratic. Reports suggested that he used psychological manipulation and coercive tactics, creating a climate of fear within the group.

Church of the First Born of the Lamb of God

DATES ACTIVE:
1970s

FOUNDERS:
Ervil LeBaron

LOCATION:
Chihuahua (Mexico)

MEMBERS:
Around 30 families

How it began

In 1890, the Church of Jesus Christ of Latter-day Saints (informally known as the Mormon Church) officially abandoned the practice of polygamy. Some polygamous Mormons moved to Mexico and were later excommunicated by the LDS Church. Ervil LeBaron's father, Alma Dayer LeBaron Sr, was one of these people, and he founded a community in Chihuahua, Mexico. When he died in 1951, leadership passed to his son Joel, who created the Church of the Firstborn of the Fulness of Times in Salt Lake City, Utah. Ervil LeBaron was second in command to Joel during the early years of the church. The group grew to include around 30 families. In 1972, the brothers clashed over leadership and went their separate ways, with Ervil starting the Church of the First Born of the Lamb of God in San Diego, California. That year, he ordered the murder of Joel, the first of many bloody acts that would characterize the history of this cult.

What did they believe?

The values of Ervil LeBaron's newly founded church were rooted in his interpretation of Mormonism. While the group shared some things in common with other fundamentalist Mormon sects, LeBaron, who claimed to be a prophet who received direct instructions from God, upheld some extreme doctrines. One of these was polygamy, which LeBaron embraced fully: he had 51 children with 13 different wives. The church also subscribed to apocalyptic beliefs, anticipating an imminent doomsday scenario. Ervil LeBaron interpreted various events and scriptures as signs of the approaching end times, reinforcing a sense of urgency and the need for strict adherence to the group's teachings. Most prominently, LeBaron introduced a discarded Mormon doctrine known as "blood atonement", which allowed for the killing of sinners to cleanse them of evil. It was this use of violence as a means of control that would lead to the group's most notorious acts: the 4 O'Clock Murders.

How it ended

Over the coming decade, Ervil LeBaron orchestrated a campaign of violent killings, most notable of which were the 4 O'Clock Murders. The targets were mainly members of his family and leaders of rival polygamous sects. On 1 June 1979, LeBaron was arrested in Mexico and extradited to the United States, where he was convicted of having ordered the murder of Rulon C. Allred, leader of the Apostolic United Brethren. In 1980, LeBaron was sentenced to life imprisonment at the Utah State Prison, where he died on 15 August 1981. And yet the killings did not stop. While in prison, LeBaron had written his 400-page "bible", *The Book of the New Covenants*, which included a commandment to kill disobedient church members named on a hit list. Three of the murders were carried out on 27 June 1988. It is thought that over 25 people were killed as a result. Many of his family members and ex-group-members would remain in hiding for years to come.

The 4 O'Clock Murders

On 27 July 1977, Rulon C. Allred, an influential leader of fundamentalist Mormon group the Apostolic United Brethren, and his bodyguard, Eddie Marston, were in Inglewood, California, to attend a court hearing related to a custody dispute. As they left the courthouse around 4 p.m., they were ambushed by members of the Church of the First Born of the Lamb of God, allegedly acting under Ervil LeBaron's orders. Allred and Marston were shot and killed. Ervil LeBaron perceived Allred as a rival and a threat to his leadership within the fundamentalist Mormon community. The 4 O'Clock Murders were a brutal and high-profile manifestation of the violent conflicts between rival factions within the hardline Mormon movement during that time. The event heightened tensions and drew public attention to the internal struggles and criminal activities associated with certain fringe Mormon groups.

Ervil LeBaron

Ervil LeBaron was born on 22 February 1925 in the Mexican state of Chihuahua and raised in a fundamentalist Mormon family which adhered to beliefs and practices outside the mainstream teachings of the church. From an early age, Ervil LeBaron expressed a deep commitment to his interpretation of Mormonism, emphasizing the practice of polygamy and a fervent anticipation of the end of the world. This apocalyptic worldview would later become a central tenet of the Church of the First Born of the Lamb of God. As he grew older, Ervil developed a conviction that he had a special calling from God and that he held a unique prophetic role in guiding his followers. These convictions would play a significant role in the formation of the Church of the First Born of the Lamb of God and its extreme doctrines.

The Family

DATES ACTIVE:
1964–1987

FOUNDERS:
Anne Hamilton-Byrne

LOCATION:
Victoria (Australia)

MEMBERS:
c. 500 at its peak

How it began

From around 1964, Anne Hamilton-Byrne ran hatha yoga classes in the suburbs of Melbourne. She recruited many of her students to join her religious and philosophical discussion group held at the home of parapsychologist Raynor Johnson. Many of the members were medical staff and psychiatrists at Newhaven Hospital in Kew. The group also recruited some of the hospital's patients. The hallucinogenic drug LSD was administered to both patients and members, and in 1968, Hamilton-Byrne began adding children to what she called "The Family". By 1975 she had acquired 14 infants and young children, some of whom were the biological children of group members, while others had been illegally adopted. There were several lawyers, doctors and social workers in the group, who were able to bypass the normal protocols relating to adoption and childcare. The cult's senior members gave children new identities by transferring to them false birth certificates or changing their names by deed poll. They were all given the surname "Hamilton-Byrne".

What did they believe?

According to The Family's philosophy, their founder, Anne Hamilton-Byrne, was the reincarnation of Jesus. Members of her inner circle claimed to be the reincarnations of Jesus's Apostles. The Family's teachings were a mix of Christianity, Hinduism and other religions. The children raised in the group were made to study the scriptures of these religions and the words of gurus such as Meher Baba, Rajneesh and Sri Chinmoy. Hamilton-Byrne's preaching often featured the concepts of karmic cleansing and immortality. She promised the adult members she recruited a chance to start afresh in the realm of life after death. In the later years of the cult, she began to predict doomsday scenarios. She said the children she had collected were her saved ones and that they would guide the planet to peace.

Children of the cult

Hamilton-Byrne's children all lived at Kai Lama, a rural property at Taylor Bay on Lake Eildon known among Family members as "Uptop". The children were kept in seclusion from the outside world and home-schooled. They were told that Hamilton-Byrne was their biological mother and that the other adults in the group were their "aunties" and "uncles". They were dressed in identical outfits, their hair all dyed peroxide blonde. Discipline in the cult was harsh. Adult cultists would beat the children regularly and subject them to other punishments such as starvation diets. When they reached adolescence, the children had to undergo an initiation process, during which the adults would give them LSD and then leave them alone in a dark room. Known as "going through", the process was supposed to help the child grow in self-awareness. In reality, it inflicted life-lasting trauma.

How it ended

One of the teenaged children, Sarah, became increasingly rebellious. In 1987, she was expelled from the group. After leaving, she met a private investigator who had been investigating The Family for years, and who revealed to her that Hamilton-Byrne was a fraud and not her real mother. Sarah played a key role in bringing the activities of The Family to the attention of the Victoria Police. On 14 August 1987, police officers raided Kai Lama and took all the children away from the premises. Hamilton-Byrne and her husband fled Australia. Six years later, they were arrested and charged with conspiracy to defraud and to commit perjury by falsely registering the births of three unrelated children as their own. These charges were later dropped. They pleaded guilty to the remaining charge of making a false declaration and were fined $5,000 each. The group went underground and existed for some years afterwards.

Anne Hamilton-Byrne

Anne Hamilton-Byrne was born Evelyn Edwards in 1921 in Sale, two hours east of Melbourne. Her father abandoned the family when Evelyn was three. Her mother, Florence Hoile, spent 27 years in mental hospitals and was known by locals as the lady who set fire to her hair in the street. As an adult, Evelyn changed her name regularly. She also altered her appearance through cosmetic surgery. By the late 1950s, she had become "Anne" and lost her first husband, Lionel Harris, in a car crash. He and Anne had been about to adopt a baby boy. She became a yoga teacher in Melbourne in the early 1960s, and it was here that she began building a following. When Hamilton-Byrne's husband died in 2001, she attended the funeral in her only public appearance following her conviction. Her final days were spent suffering from dementia in a Melbourne nursing home. She died aged 97.

Love Has Won

DATES ACTIVE:
c. 2007–2021

FOUNDERS:
Amy Carlson

LOCATION:
Colorado (US)

MEMBERS:
c. 20

How it began

In the early 2000s, Amy Carlson was working as a manager at McDonald's in Texas. Around this time she developed an interest in New Age philosophy and began regularly posting in the forums of the website Lightworkers.org. There she met Amerith WhiteEagle, who told her that she had otherworldly powers. Leaving behind her job, partner and children, she moved with him to Colorado, where they founded a group called the Galactic Federation of Light. The group posted their first videos on YouTube in 2009. Carlson was later to leave WhiteEagle, renaming the group Love Has Won. Carlson said that she was 19 billion years old, had given birth to the Universe as "Mother God" and could cure any disease, including cancer. These claims, combined with her compelling charisma, helped her to build a huge online following on Facebook and YouTube. She recruited up to 20 members who lived with her in Colorado.

What did they believe?

Carlson said that it was her mission to help the world ascend to a mystical fifth dimension. She claimed she had been reincarnated 534 times, including as Marilyn Monroe, Joan of Arc and Jesus. Love Has Won had a fluid theology that incorporated elements of New Age spirituality and mainstream Abrahamic religions. Followers also believed that Carlson was the queen of a lost continent called Lemuria, inhabitants of which lived inside Mount Shasta, California. Atlantis, the Anunnaki and "reptilians" also featured regularly in their discussions, as did conspiracy theories, with the group believing that the world was run by a "cabal" that was keeping the planet in a "low vibration" state. Other theories that they subscribed to included QAnon, which claimed that cannibalistic liberal paedophiles were plotting to overthrow Donald Trump, speculation that the COVID-19 pandemic was planned by elites and that the Sandy Hook massacre, 9/11 and the Holocaust were all hoaxes.

Life in the cult

Carlson had several romantic partners during the operational years of the cult, beginning with Amerith WhiteEagle, who was referred to as "Father God". Carlson's core group of 12–20 members lived with her in Crestone, Colorado. To generate income, the group made daily livestreams on YouTube, promoting their New Age products and so-called vitamin supplements. For $88 per session they offered a service they called "etheric surgery", in which, they alleged, sickness and "negative energy" would be removed from the client's body. Many of the videos showed how happy Carlson and the group were. But accusations and anecdotes from former members suggest things weren't quite as they seemed. There were complaints about brainwashing and members only being allowed to sleep for four to five hours a night. Drink and drugs were banned for members, and yet many former members have spoken about Carlson regularly using both and becoming abusive when under the influence.

How it ended

By September 2020, Carlson's health was deteriorating, and she stated that she had cancer. In April 2021, Saguache County Sheriff's deputies found a mummified body in a home in Crestone, Colorado, wrapped in a sleeping bag and draped with Christmas lights. The eyes were missing, a glittery powder twinkling in their place. The Mother had ascended. After Carlson's death, the group split up. The most recent "Father God", Jason Castillo, formed a separate group called Joy Rains with a small number of followers. The group took its website Lovehaswon.org offline and replaced it with a new one, 5dfulldisclosure.org. The group also renamed their Facebook page and YouTube channel to "5D Full Disclosure". In 2023, HBO released a documentary series about the cult called *Love Has Won: The Cult of Mother God*.

Amy Carlson

Amy Carlson was born in Kansas on 30 November 1975. Growing up with her sisters she seemed an ordinary child and did well at school. However, she found her parents' divorce in 1984 particularly upsetting and would go on to have a turbulent relationship with her stepmother. Carlson had been married three times by the time she was in her early twenties and had three children with three different fathers. A charismatic woman who captivated her followers, she claimed to have been reincarnated several times and to commune regularly with deceased celebrities including Robin Williams, John Lennon and Michael Jackson, whom she called "The Galactics", her spiritual ambassadors. She promoted taking colloidal silver and ingested large quantities of the substance herself. In her autopsy it emerged that this had played a key role in her health decline and death, along with other factors including alcohol abuse and anorexia.

United Nuwaubian Nation of Moors

DATES ACTIVE:

1967–present (?)

FOUNDERS:

Dwight York

LOCATION:

Georgia (US)

MEMBERS:

c. 500

How it began

Dwight York first began leading a group of Black Muslims in New York in 1967. The group's name and its teachings changed multiple times over the years, incorporating elements as diverse as Islam, Judaism, Christianity, UFO religions, New Age and many esoteric beliefs. York also changed his own name several times. In 1993, he purchased 476 acres near the town of Eatonton in Georgia, by which time the group had come to be known as the United Nuwaubian Nation of Moors (UNNM). It was here that York and his followers built a compound called "Tama-Re". York declared an affiliation with the Yamasee indigenous people and claimed that the community was descended from ancient migrants to the Americas from Egypt. The compound took on a distinct Ancient Egyptian theme, and this was also reflected in the followers' costumes for rituals and ceremonies. By 2000, the UNNM had around 500 members.

Tama-Re: a centre of controversy

On Tama-Re, most of the Nuwaubians lived in cheap trailers, but York lived in a mansion on the property. And it's not surprising he could afford it, given the amount of profit he was raking in. Various festivals were held, with one "Savior's Day" celebration in June 1998 making $500,000. Nuwaubians had to pay $25 a year for their Nuwaubian "passports", which they needed to show to enter and exit the compound. Another source of revenue was a nightclub called "Club Ramses" operated in one of the Tama-Re pyramids. This was illegal because the building had been zoned only for use as a storage facility. It was shut down by police in 1998. Relations between the group and the local authorities only worsened from there on, with various zoning disputes and altercations arising. Added to this controversy were the allegations from multiple sources that York was perpetrating crimes of sexual abuse against children in the group.

How it ended

On 8 May 2002, local police combined forces with the FBI and ATF to raid the Tama-Re compound. Fortunately, it proceeded with very little violence other than some use of tear gas by the FBI. York and his wife were arrested outside of the property. York was charged with multiple counts of child molestation and racketeering, including transport of minors for sexual use. In 2004, he was convicted by a jury in federal court and sentenced to 135 years. A subsequent appeal failed. At the time of writing, York is serving his sentence in the maximum-security prison ADX Florence in Colorado. Tama-Re was sold and the new owners demolished the buildings on the land. Following the revelations of York's misconduct, most followers abandoned the group, although some factions persisted. When York's case was considered for appeal, 200 Nuwaubians demonstrated in Atlanta to show their support.

Dwight York

Like many of the details about the Nuwaubian cult, the circumstances of Dwight York's birth are unclear. He was born on 26 June 1935 or 1945 in Boston, Massachusetts – or it could have been New Jersey, New York, Baltimore or Takoradi, Ghana. According to York, he was raised in Massachusetts, and aged seven, took a trip to Aswan, Egypt, where he learned about Islam. He claims that he returned to the United States in 1957, where he continued to study Islam. In the late 1960s, he began leading a Black Muslim group and started the organization that would eventually evolve into the UNNM. In the early 1980s, he launched a record label named Passion Productions and recorded various tracks as "Dr. York". But the record he will perhaps be most remembered for is being the subject of allegedly the largest prosecution for child molestation ever directed at a single person in the history of the United States.

DOOMSDAY
CULTS

This chapter will delve into the murky histories of organizations that were driven by the conviction that the end of the world is imminent. In these cults, prophecies of impending doom shaped the fabric of believers' lives. Such was the fervour of some followers of the Dami Mission that they went as far as to quit their jobs (be honest: would you want to spend your final days in the office?), while some members of the Church Universal and Triumphant poured all their finances into preparing for the apocalypse. Of course, when the prophesized end times fail to materialize, acolytes of these cults feel somewhat short-changed. Most such organizations tend to disband or fade away after passing their expiry date. However, others have ended on a more sinister note by dragging their members into oblivion with them.

Aum Shinrikyo

DATES ACTIVE:
1987–present

FOUNDERS:
Shoko Asahara

LOCATION:
Tokyo (Japan)

MEMBERS:
1,650

How it began

The religious movement was founded in 1987 by Shoko Asahara in Tokyo's Shibuya ward. It began life as a yoga and meditation class and gained official status as a religious organization in 1989. Initially, the cult was not associated with serious crimes, but things took a darker turn in the late 1980s, when it transpired that members were being held against their will and forced to donate money. One cult member who tried to leave in February 1989 was allegedly murdered. The group also became embroiled in a dispute with anti-cult lawyer Tsutsumi Sakamoto. In late 1989, Sakamoto, his wife and his child went missing. Their bodies were later discovered, murdered and dumped by cult members. On 27 June 1994, the cult released a cloud of sarin nerve gas in Matsumoto, Nagano, targeting the homes of judges predicted to rule against them in an ongoing real-estate dispute. Eight civilians died and 500 were injured.

What did they believe?

Aum Shinrikyo's belief system combined elements of many religions, all coloured by Asahara's idiosyncratic interpretations. In the mix were early Indian Buddhism, Tibetan Buddhism, Hinduism (with Shiva as the main image of worship), Christian millennialist ideas, the theory and practice of yoga and the writings of Nostradamus. The movement generally defined itself as an offshoot of Japanese Buddhism. In 1992, Asahara published a foundational book and declared himself to be "Christ", Japan's only fully enlightened master and the "Lamb of God". He claimed to be able to take away the sins of his followers and transfer spiritual power to them. At the heart of it all was the conviction that the apocalypse was nigh: humanity would end, except for those who joined the cult. Asahara predicted it would come in 1997 and involve the United States attacking Japan, starting World War Three.

Tokyo attack

On 20 March 1995, Aum members launched a coordinated attack on five trains in the Tokyo subway, releasing a chemical compound similar to sarin. It resulted in the deaths of 13 commuters, while 54 were seriously injured and another 980 were affected, though the true number is considered to be much higher. Asahara likely received a tip-off that police were planning to raid cult facilities and therefore ordered the attack in central Tokyo to divert police attention. However, the raids went ahead and police uncovered the full extent of the cult's activities, finding explosives, chemical weapons, a Russian Mil Mi-17 military helicopter and stockpiles of chemicals to produce enough sarin to kill 4 million people. The group denied responsibility for the attacks, saying they were conducted by members who acted secretly without consulting the group.

How it ended

A manhunt ensued. On 16 May 1995, Asahara was found hiding in the wall of a cult building and was arrested. He was charged with 23 counts of murder and 16 other offences. The trial, dubbed "the trial of the century" by the press, lasted for almost a decade. On 27 February 2004, Asahara was found guilty of masterminding the attack and was sentenced to death. Meanwhile, Aum Shinrikyo was stripped of its official "religious legal entity" status on 10 October 1995 and by early 1996 had been declared bankrupt. The group went through various transformations, re-establishing itself under the new name "Aleph" in February 2000. On 6 July 2018, Asahara and six other Aum Shinrikyo members were executed. A further six members were executed on 26 July 2018. Japan's Justice Minister Yōko Kamikawa said that the crimes "plunged people, not only in Japan but in other countries as well, into deadly fear and shook society to its core".

Shoko Asahara

Shoko Asahara was born Chizuo Matsumoto on 2 March 1955 in Kumamoto to a poor family. Partially sighted due to infantile glaucoma, he was enrolled in a school for the blind aged six. When he graduated, he went on to study acupuncture and traditional Chinese medicine, setting up a medicine shop outside Tokyo. He married and had six children. In 1981, he was convicted of practising pharmacy without a license and selling unregulated drugs. Around this time his interest in religion began in earnest and he adopted the name Shoko Asahara. In 1984, he made the first of several pilgrimages to India, where he met Tenzin Gyatso, the 14th Dalai Lama, and later said that he was given a "special mission" to preach "real Buddhism" in Japan, though the Dalai Lama denied having any significant relationship with him. He also later claimed that he had managed to achieve Enlightenment and met Shiva. He returned to Japan in 1987 and not long after founded Aum Shinrikyo.

The Movement for the Restoration of the Ten Commandments of God

DATES ACTIVE:
1989–1999

FOUNDERS:
Credonia Mwerinde and Joseph Kibweteere

LOCATION:
Southwestern Uganda

MEMBERS:
5,000

How it began

The Movement for the Restoration of the Ten Commandments of God was formed in 1989 by Credonia Mwerinde and Joseph Kibweteere. For some years already, Mwerinde had been having visions and was part of a religious group devoted to the Virgin Mary. In 1989, her father, who himself had also had visions, said she must spread the message across Uganda. That was when she met Joseph Kibweteere in Rwashamaire. He also claimed to have had a vision of the Virgin Mary in 1984, and the pair embarked on their mission to spread the Virgin's message about the apocalypse. The group's membership quickly grew. In 1992, the Rwashamaire village elders ordered the group to leave and it moved to Kanungu District, where Mwerinde's father offered an extensive property for their use. By 1997, the movement had nearly 5,000 members living communally together.

What did they believe?

The group believed that the apocalypse was coming, and that to avoid eternal damnation it was essential to obey the Ten Commandments strictly and preach the word of Jesus Christ. The adherence to the Commandments was so strong that talking was discouraged just in case someone should inadvertently break the Ninth Commandment, "Thou shalt not bear false witness against thy neighbour." Some days, communication was only conducted in sign language. There were other fastidious rules to follow: only one meal was eaten on Fridays and Mondays, sex was forbidden and so was soap. The apocalypse, according to the movement leaders, was due to occur on 31 December 1999. They wrote about this in their booklet *A Timely Message from Heaven: The End of the Present Time*, which members were required to study rigorously. The Virgin Mary was to have a special role in the end, and she communicated directly with their leaders.

How it ended

As the end of 1999 drew near, preparations went up a gear. Past members were re-recruited, and the leaders urged all to confess their sins. Clothes and cattle were sold off and work in the fields stopped. The movement was ready. New Year's Eve came around and... nothing happened. This is where things began to unravel. Members began to ask the leaders questions and payments to the group declined. Mwerinde and Kibweteere soon announced a rescheduled date for apocalypse – 17 March 2000 – and there would be a big party to celebrate. Three bulls were ordered for roasting, and 70 crates of soft drinks were brought in. Shortly after members arrived there was an explosion, and an intense fire killed all 530 present. There was no hope of escape: the doors and windows had been boarded up. A subsequent police investigation uncovered the dead bodies of around 400 more members at the movement's various properties around Uganda, most of whom had been poisoned.

Credonia Mwerinde and Joseph Kibweteere

Credonia Mwerinde, born in Uganda in 1952, was a shopkeeper, brewer of banana beer and a sex worker before she founded the Movement for the Restoration of the Ten Commandments of God with Joseph Kibweteere in 1989. Though they were joint leaders, it was said that Kibweteere was more of a figurehead, acting as a masculine presence who would uphold authority and enhance public relations. It was Mwerinde who held the true power and was the source of the predictions about the apocalypse.

Kibweteere remains somewhat of an enigma. It is known that he came from a strongly pious Catholic background. Relatively wealthy, he owned land and was able to donate some for a Catholic school that he designed himself, an action that gave him a positive image in the community at that time. He married in 1960 and ran for political office in 1980. And on 17 March 2000, both he and Mwerinde disappeared, presumed dead in the fire at the property in Kanungu.

The Dami Mission

DATES ACTIVE:
1990s

FOUNDERS:
Lee Jang Rim

LOCATION:
South Korea

MEMBERS:
c. 20,000

How it began

Details of how the South Korean Christian religious movement known as the Dami Mission came into existence are sparse, as are details about its enigmatic founder, Lee Jang Rim. The movement received worldwide attention in 1992 when Lee predicted that the rapture would occur on 28 October. The Dami Mission had over 300 churches (mostly in South Korea, but with branches in Los Angeles and New York) and 20,000 followers. When Lee announced his prediction, said to have been based on the vision of a 16-year-old boy, he claimed that 144,000 believers would ascend into heaven. Those left behind would face "seven years of war, famine and other scourges" that would obliterate all life on Earth and be followed by the Second Coming of Jesus Christ. The full details of the coming events were outlined in his book *Getting Close to the End*. Keen to get the word out, he also advertised in the *Los Angeles Times* and *The New York Times*.

The final countdown

As the calendar counted down towards 28 October, many of the 20,000 believers made extreme changes to their lives. Members gave up their homes, quit their jobs, dropped out of school and military desertions were at an all-time high. At least four followers committed suicide and one woman aborted her baby. Due to mounting pressure to do something about it, the police investigated the church and in September 1992 Lee Jang Rim was arrested for fraud. He was found to be in illegal possession of $26,711 in American currency. Other members were charged with spreading propaganda, and the police put many of the churches and certain members under surveillance. At the time, people were surprised that so many well-educated people could get swept up in such a prediction. Perhaps the hysteria reflected the underlying despair among South Koreans over relations with North Korea and ongoing domestic political unrest.

How it ended

On 28 October 1992, the Dami Mission followers were ready for the rapture. In Wonju, 54 members dressed in white burned furniture outside the Dami Mission office, while 1,000 turned up at a Dami Mission church in Seoul. Approximately 1,500 riot police and 200 detectives had taken measures to prevent mass suicides, barricading windows and stairs to the roof. Also present were 100 journalists and numerous emergency vehicles. Midnight – the moment when followers believed they would be lifted to heaven – came. Midnight passed. A teenage boy who stuck his head out of a window shouted the words that were on everyone's minds: "Nothing's happening!" And indeed, nothing did. There were no riots or further suicides. The Dami Mission was officially dissolved in November 1992 by Lee, who apologized while he was in jail awaiting sentencing. On 4 December 1992, he was convicted of fraud and sentenced to two years in prison.

The aftermath

Following the anti-climactic rapture date, many of the followers went back to their normal lives, though there were reports of some divorces among followers and two believers committed suicide. After serving his prison sentence, Lee returned to Seoul and founded a church in Mapo District. His new followers also believed in the Second Coming of Christ but did not have a specific date set for the event. In 2011, Lee and others who had made predictions about the end of the world were awarded the Ig Nobel Prize for "teaching the world to be careful when making mathematical assumptions and calculations". The Ig Nobel Prize is a satiric laurel that celebrates unusual or trivial achievements in scientific research and has been awarded annually since 1991.

Order of the Solar Temple

DATES ACTIVE:
1984–1997

FOUNDERS:
Luc Jouret and Joseph Di Mambro

LOCATION:
Saconnex d'Arve (Switzerland)

MEMBERS:
Unknown, believed to
have been in the hundreds

How it began

The Order of the Solar Temple was formed in 1984 upon the merger of two organizations, the Golden Way Foundation and the International Chivalric Order of the Solar Tradition. Luc Jouret was in charge of recruiting and instructing members, and later became the Grand Master, while Di Mambro took control of finance and was the organization's true leader. In 1985, Di Mambro set up a survival centre in Canada in the event of nuclear war. The cult also owned various properties around France and Switzerland. It wasn't long before disagreements erupted in the leadership, with senior members accusing Di Mambro of deceit and embezzlement. Di Mambro and Jouret argued about the dissemination of the cult's beliefs and teachings. In the early 1990s, Di Mambro changed tack with his teachings and began to preach about a transit to another planet called Sirius. He told certain members that one day they would be called to a meeting to accomplish the transit and that they should be on 24-hour alert.

What did they believe?

The cult claimed that their belief system was based upon the ideals of the Knights Templar. The members saw themselves as assisting in the arrival of the coming New Age and held a complex set of esoteric beliefs that blended Christianity, UFO conspiracy theories and elements of occultism. Central to their doctrine was the notion of reincarnation and the cyclical nature of human existence. Adherents trusted in the existence of extraterrestrial beings who would assist them in transcending to a higher plane of being. The cult's leaders claimed to be the earthly representatives of divine entities and promised followers an idyllic afterlife on a mythical planet. The group also held that a forthcoming generation of extraordinary children, including nine cosmic offspring, would usher in the New Age. In pursuit of this, Di Mambro identified group members with renowned figures from their past lives and orchestrated "cosmic marriages" between them.

Ritual

Rituals formed a big part of the order's meetings. Involving a fusion of Christian symbols and occult practices, they were seen as facilitating the spiritual journey and preparing members for the impending cosmic transit. The lodges where the members met had altars and members wore costumes – often a white robe with a red cross to signify the Knights Templar. They practised various meditative and occult disciplines to achieve an enlightened state of consciousness. The organization had a labyrinthine structure and, as members progressed through the hierarchy, they took part in elaborate initiation ceremonies, for which they had to buy expensive jewellery, costumes and regalia, and pay initiation fees. Many members reported seeing supernatural apparitions during ritual ceremonies. However, these were likely the results of fakery enacted by Di Mambro and his wife Jocelyne behind the scenes.

How it ended

In 1994, the first of three "transits" was enacted. During these transits, members would escape to a higher world through suicide. Others would be murdered for being traitors to the order. The first to go were two parents and their baby, who Di Mambro believed to be the antichrist. They were murdered in Quebec in September. In October, in Quebec and Switzerland, 53 members died either by murder (they were stabbed or poisoned) or suicide (from taking sedatives). The two properties in Switzerland were set on fire and many bodies were burned beyond recognition. Jouret and Di Mambro's bodies were identified by their dental records. In 1995, 16 bodies were found in Vercors, France. Finally, in 1997 in Quebec, there were five more suicides. They left behind a letter explaining that they had taken this action to ensure a path to the new world.

Luc Jouret and Joseph Di Mambro

Born on 18 October 1947 in the Belgian Congo, Jouret later moved to Belgium when his parents returned there. He attended the Free University of Brussels and became a physician. He had a brief spell in the army, then trained as a homeopathic physician and set up a practice in France. In the early 1980s, he made a name for himself as a speaker on alternative medicine and travelled throughout French-speaking Europe and Quebec.

Born on 19 August 1924 in France, Di Mambro grew up to become a jeweller and watchmaker. As a young man he joined the Ancient and Mystical Order of the Rosae Crucis (AMORC). He was passionate about esoteric beliefs and became a full-time lecturer in the New Age Movement. In 1973, he founded the Center for the Preparation of the New Age, in Annemasse, France, which was succeeded by the Golden Way Foundation.

True Russian Orthodox Church

DATES ACTIVE:
Unknown–2008

FOUNDERS:
Pyotr Kuznetsov

LOCATION:
Penza region (Russia)

MEMBERS:
c. 35

How it began

The True Russian Orthodox Church, also known as the Penza Recluses, was founded by Pyotr Kuznetsov. The independent doomsday cult broke away from the Russian Orthodox Church, considering it insufficiently orthodox. Its members lived under a strict set of rules and were not allowed to watch television, handle money or eat processed food. They rejected anything that contained numbers, such as barcodes, national identification numbers and passports, because they said they held satanic symbols, or "the number of the Beast". In November 2007, Kuznetsov told the group to hide themselves away and await the end of the world, which he predicted would take place in May 2008. And so between 29 and 35 members of the group holed themselves up in a cave, near the village Nikolskoye in Russia's Penza region. Kuznetsov did not go with the group, saying that God had given him different tasks. The group members in the cave threatened to commit suicide en masse if the authorities tried to intervene.

How it ended

The group kept this up for months, sticking out the unpleasant conditions in the winter-bound cave for as long as they could. But there was only so much they could take. On 28 March 2008, seven female members emerged and were treated by emergency workers. Three days later, melting snow caused part of the cave to collapse and a further 14 members left. On 16 May 2008, the last nine members of the cult exited the cave. They could no longer tolerate the toxic fumes emitted from the corpses of two cult members who had died over winter. The authorities removed the dead bodies and on 21 May they blew the cave up, as it was a danger to the local population and any curious visitors. After leaving the cave, most of the sect members left Nikolskoye, except for one family. Vasily Nedogon, the head of that family, continued to live there with his wife and three children without electricity and passports, awaiting the end time that he believed would come soon.

Pyotr Kuznetsov

Little is known about Pyotr Kuznetsov, the leader of the True Russian Orthodox Church, or "Heavenly Jerusalem", as the group was also known. The 43-year-old divorced engineer (or architect, depending on accounts) declared himself a prophet, having come from a religious family. Several years before the cave incident he left his family and travelled across Belarus and Russia, touring monasteries, writing books and spreading his message of apocalyptic doom before settling in the village of Nikolskoye. There were some reports that Kuznetsov suffered from schizophrenia and others that he spent several months sleeping in a coffin. One thing everyone agreed on was that he was clearly suffering from mental health issues. On 3 April 2008, Kuznetsov attempted suicide and was taken to a psychiatric hospital. In subsequent years, he was diagnosed with paranoia and remained in psychiatric care, with the court extending the period of his compulsory treatment in 2016.

Church Universal and Triumphant

DATES ACTIVE:

1975–present

FOUNDERS:

Elizabeth Clare Prophet

LOCATION:

Montana (US)

MEMBERS:

Between 30,000 and 50,000 members
in the United States and abroad

How it began

The Church Universal and Triumphant's (CUT) influences stretch back to two earlier religious movements, Theosophy and I AM. Theosophy centred around the idea of receiving teachings from spiritual adepts known as the Masters. I AM adopted the idea of Ascended Masters and taught that they had sent a message that a new golden age of humanity would begin in the United States. In 1958, Mark Prophet, who had been involved in I AM and claimed to be a Messenger in direct contact with the Ascended Masters, founded The Summit Lighthouse. In 1961, he married Elizabeth Clare Prophet, whom he announced was also a Messenger. When Mark died in 1975, Elizabeth took over the organization, renaming it the Church Universal and Triumphant. She moved its headquarters from Colorado Springs to southern California in 1976 and then to its present location in Montana in 1986. In the 1980s, the church faced a lot of opposition from the anti-cult movement, especially the Cult Awareness Network.

What did they believe?

The church's beliefs were centred around the I AM, or God Presence, the innate spark of divinity in every individual. Those who reached their full potential became Ascended Masters and could assist humanity. I AM presented Jesus as an Ascended Master and identified as part of the Judeo-Christian tradition. It also believed in reincarnation, and that individuals could break the cycle and access the divine realms through ascension. The church was millenarian and claimed that the Ascended Masters' plan for humanity was being countered by "Dark Forces" or "Fallen Ones" believed to be acting through communism, left-wing groups and elite power brokers. They claimed there was a global growth in negative karma in a build-up towards the end of the Piscean Age and its replacement with the Aquarian Age. The church hoped that the apocalypse could be averted through prayers but also made preparations for survival, in the hope of emerging from the aftermath to build a new age.

Preparing for the end

The ranch in Montana, where the group settled in 1986, was envisioned as a place where members could live off the land after the end, which Prophet predicted would come in the form of a nuclear apocalypse on 15 March 1990. The church acquired 30,000 acres of land and started construction of an underground nuclear shelter. The group began stockpiling enough food and supplies to last up to seven years. In July 1989, one senior church member was arrested after trying to buy weapons under a false name. Locals were concerned the group were planning an attack. They were also worried about the environmental impact of the group's activities on nearby Yellowstone National Park after the church's storage tanks leaked 21,000 gallons of diesel and 11,500 gallons of gasoline in April 1990. In early March that year, church members began arriving at the ranch, with around 7,000 members entering the shelters on 15 March.

How it ended

On 16 March 1990, members emerged from the shelter. The nuclear apocalypse had not occurred. About a third of the congregation left the church immediately. Many of them had left their jobs and spent their savings buying survival supplies, leaving them broke. Elizabeth Prophet was ready with an answer for why the nuclear attack had not occurred: the church's prayers had averted the disaster. In 1996, several Church members split to form their own group and Prophet announced that she was transferring her leadership role to Gilbert Cleirbaut. The church leaders led a complete reorganization of the church, decentralizing it and greatly reducing the numbers of the community stationed at its headquarters. In 1999, Prophet announced that she had Alzheimer's disease and retired from leadership. Over the coming years, the church slowly split into further splinter groups.

Elizabeth Clare Prophet

Elizabeth Clare Prophet was born in Long Branch, New Jersey on 8 April 1939. She claimed to have had several mystical experiences while growing up, including a vision of herself playing on the sands of the Nile river in Egypt, which her mother told her was a memory from a past life. On another occasion, while water-skiing, she described feeling suspended above a place filled with joyous spiritual beings who radiated love. She moved to Boston in 1959, where she worked as a secretary for the Christian Science church and *The Christian Science Monitor*. The knowledge and experience she gained there would help her later in running her own church. It was also where she met her first husband, Mark L. Prophet. Diagnosed with Alzheimer's disease in November 1998, Prophet died on 15 October 2009 in Bozeman, Montana.

Chen Tao

DATES ACTIVE:
1993–1998

FOUNDERS:
Hon-Ming Chen

LOCATION:
Taiwan and US

MEMBERS:
c. 140–160

How it began

Chen Tao, also known as God's Salvation Church, began life in the early 1990s in Taiwan. Hon-Ming Chen, who had joined a UFO-oriented religious group in 1992, became disillusioned because the leaders took payment for their teachings. He accused them of being part devil and left the group with some other followers with whom he founded the Soul Light Resurgence Association (SLRA) in 1993. Chen began to preach that North America is the "Pureland of God". In 1996, he self-published a book entitled *The Practical Evidence and Study of the World of God and Buddha*, explaining his worldview and religious ideas, in which he advocated that followers of God's message should move to the United States to survive the coming "Great Tribulation". The group moved to San Dimas, Los Angeles in 1997, then a few months later relocated to Garland, Texas.

What did they believe?

The new religious movement's beliefs were a combination of Buddhism, Taoism, Christian millennialism and ufology. According to Chen, much of the world is dominated by evil spirits. He called himself a prophet and claimed that he was able to chart the course of individual salvation. In Garland, Texas, he self-published a second book, *God's Descending on Clouds (Flying Saucers) to Save People*, which stated that God would descend in human form at the group's residence in Garland on 31 March 1998. The human incarnation of God would physically resemble Chen, be able to speak all languages and walk through walls. Six days before this date, on 25 March, God would announce his descent on Channel 18, broadcast across North America.

The hunt for Canadian Jesus

The group's unusual beliefs were not confined to Chen's prophecy of God's first live TV broadcast. In June 1997, Chen and a small group of his followers set out on a search mission in Vancouver, Canada. They were looking for the "Jesus of the West", about whom Chen had received information in a vision and had foretold in *The Practical Evidence and Study of the World of God and Buddha*. According to Chen, there were two spiritual light bodies of Jesus Christ; one was born in Taiwan and the other in Canada. The Canadian "reincarnation of Jesus" would be a 28-year-old six-foot tall man who looked like Abraham Lincoln and would be found living in Vancouver. To track down the Canadian Christ, Chen's group placed a personal advertisement in *The Province* and *Vancouver Sun*. They received no responses to the advertisement.

How it ended

In the run up to 25 March 1998, the Garland Police Department, concerned that the group could be planning a mass suicide attempt, had their forces on standby and the international media began to gather outside the group's residence. Group members prepared themselves in a baptism-like ritual, wading in the creek behind the residence, while some members shaved their heads. On 25 March, a huge crowd gathered outside the house. But at midnight, the moment of the expected broadcast, there was nothing but static on Channel 18. Shortly after this, Chen issued a press release, maintaining that everyone should still prepare for God's appearance on 31 March. Once again, the crowd was disappointed. Chen offered to be stoned or crucified in recompense for the no-show, but no one took him up on the offer. Following the failed prediction, Chen Tao effectively fell apart, with around two-thirds of members abandoning the group, while the rest later moved to New York.

Hon-Ming Chen

Hon-Ming Chen was born on 22 April 1955 in Chiayi, Taiwan. While his parents were Buddhist, they also observed many customs of Chinese folk religion, though religion was not a prominent focus in their home life. Chen graduated with a bachelor's degree in political science and in 1983 got a job as an associate professor at Chia Nan Junior College of Pharmacy, where he taught social science until 1993. Hon-Ming Chen identified himself as an atheist for most of his life, but in 1992 he claimed that he received a message from God instructing him to follow a religious life. He began studying various religious texts such as the Buddhist Sutras, the New and Old Testaments, and the Tao Te Ching. He studied under various New Age teachers and became a student of a UFO religious group in 1992, before leaving to form his own group and eventually going on to found God's Salvation Church.

SEX CULTS

Regular orgies. Hedonistic parties. Bizarre sex rituals. Free love and nudity for all. On the surface, a sex cult might sound like the most fun type to join out of those featured in this book. But you only need scratch the surface to reveal the disturbing truth. As it turns out, when spirituality and sexuality meet, a lot can go wrong. Many of the cults in this chapter used sex to psychologically manipulate and control their members. In several of them, sexual abuse was common: of both adults and children. Some of these cults ostensibly used sex as a way to attract new members, while with others sex was not officially a part of their practices but they have been included because sexual abuse was so rife in their ranks.

The Children of God

DATES ACTIVE:

1968–1977
(still active under the title
The Family International)

FOUNDERS:

David Brandt Berg

LOCATION:

Huntington Beach, California (US)

MEMBERS:

Unknown, thought to be tens of thousands

How it began

In 1968, former Christian and Missionary Alliance pastor David Brandt Berg founded a group known as Teens for Christ who would gather at a coffeehouse in Huntington Beach, California. After having a premonition that California would be affected by a major earthquake, he took his followers on the road, where they preached and distributed pamphlets. While they were camped in Lewis and Clark Park, a news reporter first called them "The Children of God". Berg communicated with his followers primarily by writing letters, known as "Mo Letters", of which he published nearly 3,000 over the next 24 years. He styled himself as God's prophet for the contemporary world. By 1972, the group had established 130 communities around the world, and by the mid-1970s, it had "colonies" in approximately 70 countries with an estimated 10,000 full-time members.

What did they believe?

The group's beliefs were rooted in a unique interpretation of Christianity. Their teachings were apocalyptic, foretelling the rise of a brutal One World Government with a dictatorial Antichrist at its head, which would eventually be overthrown in the Second Coming of Jesus Christ. But The Children of God would offer salvation, spiritual revolution and happiness. They emphasized communal living and rejected traditional societal norms, referring to the world outside their communes as "The System". In 1976, Berg introduced a new recruitment method called Flirty Fishing, in which female members were encouraged to show "God's love" by having sex with potential members. Berg held the philosophy that God was love and love was sex, and sex shouldn't be limited by relationship or age. Given this sexual climate, it should come as no great surprise that the cult has been the focus of numerous allegations of child abuse.

God's children

Several ex-members who grew up in The Children of God later became celebrities, while others have publicly spoken out about what went on in the cult and published books about their experiences. These include:

- 👁 Rose McGowan's father ran a chapter of the cult in Italy. She described her experiences in interviews with Howard Stern in *People* magazine and published a book about them called *Brave*.

- 👁 River Phoenix, along with his siblings Joaquin, Rain, Liberty and Summer, was part of the group from 1972 to 1978. River told *Details* magazine in November 1991 that "they're ruining people's lives".

- 👁 Ex-members Celeste Jones, Kristina Jones and Juliana Buhring co-authored *Not Without My Sister*, which gives details of the abuse they experienced in the cult.

How it ended

The Children of God was abolished in February 1978, but things didn't end there. Berg conducted a major reorganization of the movement and renamed it "The Family of Love". He dismissed over 300 leading members due to "reports of serious misconduct and abuse of their positions". The majority of the group's beliefs remained the same. The organization was later renamed The Family (1982–2003) and finally The Family International (2004–present). In March 1989, The Family issued a statement that in "early 1985" a message had been sent to all members in reference to adult-child sexual contact, "reminding them that any such activities are strictly forbidden within our group". Anyone found to be involved in such activities, they said, would be excommunicated.

David Brandt Berg

David Brandt Berg was born on 18 February 1919 in Oakland, California. His parents were Christian evangelists and he spent his early years moving around the country with them. His parents depended on the generosity of their parishioners and lived frugally, which became a lifelong habit for Berg that he encouraged in his followers. He studied at Monterey High School and Elliott School of Business Administration, and in the late 1940s became a minister in the Christian and Missionary Alliance. He was later expelled from the organization for alleged sexual misconduct with a church employee. Berg ran a branch of his friend Fred Jordan's Soul Clinic in Miami, Florida, as a missionary training school, but he got into trouble with local authorities because of his outspoken disapproval of evolution being taught as fact in public schools. He and his family moved to Texas and later to Huntington Beach, California, where he set up what was to become The Children of God.

Fundamentalist Church of Jesus Christ of Latter-Day Saints

DATES ACTIVE:
1929–present

FOUNDERS:
Lorin C. Woolley

LOCATION:
Various locations around the US

MEMBERS:
Estimated 10,000

How it began

The Fundamentalist Church of Jesus Christ of Latter-Day Saints (FLDS) is a radical polygamist sect that splintered off from The Church of Jesus Christ of Latter-Day Saints (LDS Church, also known as the Mormon Church) after it renounced the practice of polygamy in 1890. Polygamy is illegal in all 50 states of the US. It all began in Short Creek (now Colorado City), where members of the Mormon community continued with their polygamist ways, attracting a larger following of other LDS ex-members. In 1953, as part of a government crackdown on polygamy, all the FLDS Church members of Short Creek, including 236 children, were arrested in the Short Creek raid. And yet polygamists continued to live in the community established there. In September 2002, Warren Jeffs became the leader of the movement. An enthusiastic polygamist, he swiftly married all of his deceased father's wives (he's thought to have around 70).

What do they believe?

The FLDS adheres to many of the same beliefs as the standard LDS Church from which it originated. One key difference is that the FLDS follows the tenet that faithful men must follow what is known as the doctrine of plural marriage. There is a strong emphasis on the concept of "celestial marriage", a belief that these nuptials are essential for reaching the highest level of heaven. Warren Jeffs' own slant on this was that devoted church members should have at least three wives to get into heaven. And furthermore, that the more wives a man has, the closer he is to heaven. The FLDS is led by a prophet, who is considered a spiritual and temporal leader, and his authority is believed to be divinely sanctioned. Leadership passes from one prophet to another, with Jeffs having inherited the role from his father.

Life inside "The Creek"

The FLDS community is made up of the twin towns of Colorado City and Hildale, which straddle the state line between Arizona and Utah. Around 10,000 people are believed to live in the community, which is known to its members as "The Creek" after the original location of Short Creek. Much of what goes on there is kept secret, but ex-members have leaked some details. Most forms of entertainment are banned, including toys, television, the internet, birthday and Christmas celebrations, festivals, parades, camping and fishing. Women's bodies are considered sacred temples and must be covered from neck to ankles, and women never cut their hair because, so the teachings say, they must use it in heaven to wash men's feet. Underground the north end of the community lies an abandoned network of tunnels cut into the mountainside as an escape route in the event of a government raid.

How it ended

Following multiple allegations of sexual assault and abuse, in 2005, Warren Jeffs was eventually charged with sexual assault on a minor, among other crimes, and a warrant was put out for his arrest. Further allegations came to light and additional charges were made, and in 2006, the FBI placed Jeffs on its Top Ten Most Wanted Fugitives list. A $60,000 reward was offered, shortly raised to $100,000. He was finally arrested when a highway trooper pulled him over because the temporary licence plates on his car were not displayed properly. In 2011, he was sentenced for sexually assaulting two underage girls who were two of his many "wives". At the time of writing, he is still serving life plus 20 years in a Texas state prison. Jeffs formally resigned as President of the FLDS Church on 20 November 2007. However, he is still viewed by many in the community to be the prophet, and these followers continue to pray for his release.

Warren Jeffs

Warren Jeffs was born on 3 December 1955 in Sacramento, California, to Rulon Jeffs and Marilyn Steed. His father, Rulon, was the leader and "prophet" of the FLDS. Warren grew up near Salt Lake City, Utah. In 1976, he became principal of Alta Academy, an FLDS private school, where he was known for being a strict disciplinarian. When his father passed away, he became the president and prophet of the FLDS. Over the years Jeffs amassed a great fortune, most of which was made through real estate and construction, with him supposedly owning $100 million worth of property by 2006. Apparently, he used his followers for free or low-cost labour on his construction projects. In July 2004, Brent Jeffs, Jeffs' nephew, alleged that Jeffs had raped him in the late 1980s. There followed a great many other allegations of sexual violence from other family members and his underage wives, eventually leading to his arrest and sentencing on related charges.

Goel Ratzon

DATES ACTIVE:
1991–2009

FOUNDERS:
Goel Ratzon

LOCATION:
Tel Aviv (Israel)

MEMBERS:
21

How it began

From around 1991, Ratzon became famous in Tel Aviv as a spiritual healer. He married many women, put them together in several houses and had children with them. In each house, domestic duties were shared between the women and Ratzon would visit periodically, choosing one of his wives to spend the night with him. Nine of his sons and daughters with these women were named after him. In February 2009, Israeli journalists Shelley Tapiro and Nesli Barda received permission from Ratzon to film inside one of the houses. The footage was aired by Israeli TV Channel 10. A day after the broadcast, Ratzon gave an interview with Israeli TV Channel 2, during which he claimed that he had only assisted women who needed his help. The broadcasts catapulted Ratzon into the public eye and many called his community a cult. Ratzon and his wives, however, called it a "cooperative" and compared it to the Kibbutzim set up during the establishment of Israel.

Life in the cult

Ratzon wrote a document containing a set of rules called "The Book of the Family", which all of his wives had to read once a week and keep in strictest secrecy. In the document, Ratzon referred to himself as God and to his children as "Sons of God". The rules covered the education of the children, daily housekeeping and sexual relations with Ratzon. The women had to dress modestly. It was forbidden for them to look at or talk to other men, and neither could they touch each other or other women. Smoking, drinking alcohol and eating meat were all banned. The majority of Ratzon's wives were no longer in touch with their families, who did not approve of them being in the cult. Some of their families hired private investigators to find out information about Ratzon and what was going on in his households. They filed complaints against him, without any success.

How it ended

It wasn't all happy families in the houses of Ratzon. One of his wives called Galit, whose two sisters were also part of his cult, left him and filed a complaint with the police against him for raping her when she was 14. The police began surveillance of the Ratzon households. In one recorded conversation, Ratzon was heard mentioning that he had sexual intercourse with one of his daughters. On 12 January 2010, Ratzon was arrested on suspicion of slavery and sexual assault against minors. Following his arrest, the wives and children were taken from Ratzon's houses to a women's shelter. Four years later, he was convicted of most of the sexual assaults with which he had been charged, but acquitted of the slavery charge, and was sentenced to prison for 30 years. He filed for appeal, but this was denied.

Goel Ratzon

Goel Ratzon was born on 19 September 1950 in Hatikva Quarter, Tel Aviv. His parents had immigrated to Israel from Yemen. In 1972, he married and had five children. By the early 1980s, he had met and had five more children with another woman. And he was only just getting started. He is thought to eventually have had 21 wives and 49 children. During the operational years of his cult, his income came from funds transferred to him by his wives. Ratzon claimed that he had romantic relationships with all his wives. Whether or not this is true, he certainly held great influence and power over them. Some of his wives said they adored him and even tattooed his name and likeness on their arms. They called him the Messiah. Publicly, Ratzon tried to distance himself from this imagery. He said that their gratitude to him was only in response to what he had given them.

Rajneesh movement

DATES ACTIVE:
1974–present

FOUNDERS:
Bhagwan Shree Rajneesh
(also known as Osho)

LOCATION:
Pune (India) and Antelope, Oregon (US)

MEMBERS:
c. 30–50,000

How it began

Indian mystic and spiritual leader Bhagwan Shree Rajneesh, also known as Osho in later life, began to initiate people into his order of neo-sannyasins (new followers) in the early 1970s. In 1974, he set up the movement's headquarters in Pune, India, and later expanded the movement into other locations around the world. In 1981, Rajneesh set up a community known as Rajneeshpuram in Antelope, Oregon, which became its global headquarters. By this stage, the movement had various investments and holdings, and was receiving large numbers of donations from followers, generating millions of dollars every year. From 1982 an annual World Festival was held at Rajneeshpuram, attended by around 15,000 people in 1984, when it made nearly $10 million. Thousands of followers called the ranch home, and it had its own fire department, police, restaurants, malls, airstrip and public transport system.

What did they believe?

Traditionally, the sannyasis practised asceticism, avoiding all forms of self-indulgence, but Rajneesh taught his followers to live fully. He believed everyone could find their own way to spiritual enlightenment and advocated a communal, pastoral and spiritual way of life. Rajneesh was a huge promoter of sexual liberation. He encouraged his followers to forgo marriage and supported contraception and abortion, wanting to prevent the birth of children in his communes. He wanted everyone to embrace free love. This gave rise to a certain amount of sexual hedonism at the ranch, which was a huge draw for new recruits. Rajneesh believed that inner freedom could be attained by first accepting and then surpassing one's desires. He also praised capitalism and consumption, saying that poverty only existed in the world because religions praised poverty. His followers wore ochre-coloured robes and a mala (a necklace of 108 beads) with a photograph of Rajneesh.

Trouble at the ranch

Rajneeshpuram had been built on land that had been zoned for agricultural purposes, and according to regulations only six residents were allowed to live there. But there was a huge number of people living there, which led to complaints from local residents. When inspectors visited, Rajneesh told them the ranch was an agricultural cooperative. He was instructed that the non-farm uses of the land should be relocated in an urban area, and so the movement began purchasing property in the nearby town of Antelope. Local residents tried but failed to disincorporate the city of Antelope. Many Rajneeshees were now citizens of Antelope, and eventually they took control of the city council. After an attempt to change the town name to Rajneesh, tensions escalated between the mostly Christian locals and the Rajneeshees.

How it ended

Things came to a head in 1984. Not content with running the council, the Rajneeshees wanted to control Wasco County, home to the ranch and town, and so they targeted the voting population of The Dalles, Oregon. They did so by contaminating the salad bars at almost a dozen local restaurants with salmonella. More than 700 people became ill, though luckily there were no fatalities. In the ensuing federal investigation, two senior Rajneeshees were convicted with masterminding the attack and served jail time. Rajneesh attempted to flee the country but was arrested in North Carolina and subsequently charged. He was deported and returned to his Pune ashram in India. Rajneeshpuram soon became a ghost town. Following Rajneesh's death in 1990, the Pune ashram in India was renamed the Osho Institute and later the Osho International Meditation Resort. It still attracts hundreds of thousands of visitors every year.

Bhagwan Shree Rajneesh

Bhagwan Shree Rajneesh was born on 11 December 1931 as Chandra Mohan Jain in the village of Kuchwada, in the state of what is now Madhya Pradesh in India. As a young man he spent time learning from various religious leaders around India. At the age of 21, he had an intense spiritual awakening, which led him to the realization that individual religious experience is the central fact of spiritual life. Such experiences, he held, cannot be organized into any single belief system. He studied philosophy at the University of Jabalpur, graduating with a BA in 1955 and going on to earn an MA from the University of Saugar. He took up a teaching post at the University of Jabalpur in 1957. He resigned in 1966, focusing his efforts on becoming a guru and meditation guide. In the early 1970s he began initiating people into the order of sannyasis, which in turn led to his founding the Rajneesh movement.

Church of the Most High Goddess

DATES ACTIVE:
1987–1989

FOUNDERS:
Mary Ellen and Wilbur Tracy

LOCATION:
Los Angeles, California (US)

MEMBERS:
c. 2,000

How it began

Mary Ellen and Wilbur Tracy were practising Mormons who raised their seven children in the faith. After doing some research, Mary Ellen reported to the church leaders that she had discovered obscure teachings that allowed married women to have extramarital sex. The Mormon leaders rejected her suggestion and promptly excommunicated the couple. The couple did some research into the history of sexuality and spirituality and in 1987 founded the Church of the Most High Goddess. Mary Ellen, who filled the role of high priestess, took the sacred name of "Sabrina Aset". They converted a four-bedroom house in West Los Angeles into a temple, adorning it with Egyptian symbols and a large nude portrait of Mary. Ready for their first communicant, the church placed advertisements in *The Hollywood Express*, an adult-oriented weekly tabloid, featuring nude photos of Mary Ellen, explaining the beliefs of the church and promising "hedonistic religious rituals".

What they believed

Through their research, the Tracys concluded that the purest form of religion is Goddess spirituality, in which a female deity is worshipped and sex is a sacrament. They sought to revive the worship of the ancient Egyptian goddess Isis. As high priestess of the church, Mary Ellen's divine duties included engaging in sexual intercourse with the congregants. According to her, she had sex with over 2,000 men as part of a ritual of spiritual cleansing, and with a great many women too. Before undertaking the cleansing ritual, supplicants would receive religious instruction and an assessment of their readiness to undergo the ritual.

The 537th High Priestess

Mary Ellen claimed to be the 537th High Priestess in a line of temple courtesans tracing back to 3200 BC in Egypt, of which Cleopatra was number 469. She described her work as follows:

"In my calling as a priestess, I have sex with men of all sizes, shapes, colours, backgrounds, professions. To date I've had vaginal sex with over 2,779 different men, oral sex with over 4,000 different men, and […] a couple of hundred [women] along the way. Since I'm a very sexual person, I've had sex, not just in the religious rituals, but in a wide variety of places in addition to the usual bedrooms, sofas, chairs and back and front seats of cars – like doctor's [sic] examination tables, college professor's [sic] offices, faculty lounges, dormitories, showers, swimming pools, Jacuzzi [sic], beaches, woods, tents, campers, business offices, back rooms of stores, warehouses, rest rooms, government offices, parking lots, trucks, elevators, on the hood of cars, in adult films – on and off camera."

A sacred ritual

The spiritual cleansing ritual had four parts:

1. Confession

   The supplicant would confess and be expected to make restitution where possible.

2. Dedication

   In a simulation of the birth position, the supplicant would place his/her head between the legs of the priestess and perform cunnilingus.

3. Sacrifice

   The supplicant would need to make a donation called a tithe (10 per cent) of their time or worth.

4. Purification

   Male supplicants would have vaginal intercourse with the priestess, preparing for godhood in the after world by giving up their essence (semen) to the priestess (as personification of the goddess). This stage would be modified for female supplicants.

How it ended

The church caught the attention of the police after it was featured in a series of articles in the local paper and on the *Sally Jessy Raphael Show* on TV, where mention was made of the "Sacrifice", which consisted of a mandatory $100–$200 cash donation made by supplicants. In April 1989, an undercover officer visited the temple, where, he later testified, Mary Ellen solicited him for oral sex in exchange for a $150 donation. He refused to pay and was asked to leave. Vice officers then raided the temple. Mary Ellen was charged with prostitution and Wilbur Tracy with procurement. They were convicted and sentenced to jail time of one year and six months, respectively. In a separate legal battle, they took the Los Angeles County District Attorney to court, hoping to secure a legal exemption to the anti-prostitution laws. The Tracys did not win their suit.

Mary Ellen Tracy

Mary Ellen Tracy, also known as Sabrina Aset, was born in 1943. She completed a degree in chemistry at the University of Miami and did graduate work in the same discipline at UCLA. She also held a Master's in environmental sciences/chemistry from Portland State University. She was raised a Mormon and practised the religion until being excommunicated in the 1980s. During the early 1990s, she hosted her own public-access television talk show series called *Sabrina On...* where she discussed subjects ranging from religious freedom to gender-changing, and publicized the Church of the Most High Goddess. She also occasionally danced on camera wearing nothing but Egyptian-style jewellery. Under various stage names, she also played a role in several X-rated films, including the *Positively Pagan* series and *Club Head 2* (1991). No stranger to the limelight, she also appeared in a television broadcast of *Donahue* and on *The Montel Williams Show*.

Conclusion

And so concludes this journey through the weird and, at times, downright disturbing world of cults. Whether they are best known for their esoteric religious beliefs, their doomsday predictions or their unusual sexual practices, all the cults in this book have something in common: their charismatic leaders with an unstoppable will to control others.

Some of the cults were started with genuine good intentions to make the world a better place and assist their members on their spiritual journey. But when excessive dedication to an ideology or person comes into play, especially when combined with unethical leadership that relies on psychological manipulation, things rarely end well for anyone involved.

Being little in nature, this book has only covered some of the many cults to have existed, and of those featured, it has given an overview of what in most cases is a complex, messy and contradictory history. If you would like to delve into more detail on any of the cults featured, or to discover more cults to shock and appal you, refer to the Further Reading section, where you will find many avenues to continue your learning.

Further Reading

General books about cults:

Max Cutler, *Cults: Inside the World's Most Notorious Groups and Understanding the People Who Joined Them* (2022)

Robert Jay Lifton, *Losing Reality: On Cults, Cultism, and the Mindset of Political and Religious Zealotry* (2019)

Amanda Montell, *Cultish: The Language of Fanaticism* (2021)

Paul Morantz and Hal Lancaster, *Escape: My Life-Long War Against Cults* (2012)

Rick Alan Ross, *Cults Inside Out: How People Get In and Can Get Out* (2014)

Books about specific cults:

N. Jamiyla Chisholm, *The Community* (2022)

Clive Doyle, Catherine Wessinger and Matthew D. Wittmer, *A Journey to Waco* (2012)

Tim Guest, *My Life in Orange* (2004)

Rachel Jeffs, *Breaking Free: How I Escaped Polygamy, the FLDS Cult, and My Father, Warren Jeffs* (2017)

Deborah Layton, *Seductive Poison: A Jonestown Survivor's Story of Life and Death in the Peoples Temple* (1998)

Haruki Murakami, *Underground: The Tokyo Gas Attack and the Japanese Psyche* (1997)

Deb Simpson, *Closing the Gate* (2012)

Natacha Tormey, *Born Into the Children of God: My Life in a Religious Sex Cult and My Struggle for Survival on the Outside* (2014)

TV documentaries:

Children of God
Heaven's Gate: The Cult of Cults
Jonestown: The Women Behind the Massacre
Kumaré
Love Has Won: The Cult of Mother God
Prophet's Prey
Sons of Perdition
The Family
Waco: The Rules of Engagement
Wild Wild Country

Podcasts:

IndoctriNation, hosted by Rachel Bernstein
Let's Talk About Sects, hosted by Sarah Steel
Trust Me, hosted by Lola Blanc and Meagan Elizabeth

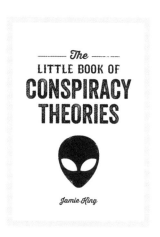

The Little Book of Conspiracy Theories

A Pocket Guide to the World's Greatest Mysteries

Jamie King

Paperback • ISBN: 978-1-83799-436-6

The curious world of conspiracy theories is unbelievable and scarily believable in equal measure. *The Little Book of Conspiracy Theories* is an insight into this shocking and mysterious world. Discover how popular theories originated and took root, what they claim, and how "the truth" has been covered up with this introductory guide.

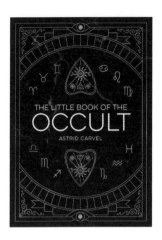

The Little Book of the Occult

An Introduction to Dark Magick

Astrid Carvel

Paperback • ISBN: 978-1-80007-722-5

Occult practices are no longer associated with summoning evil entities – they're a fun and insightful way to achieve your dreams, discover more about yourself and others, and feel empowered. *The Little Book of the Occult* offers an introduction to this fascinating subject, exploring its rich history and numerous potential benefits.

Have you enjoyed this book?
If so, find us on Facebook at
SUMMERSDALE PUBLISHERS, on Twitter/X at
@SUMMERSDALE and on Instagram and TikTok
at **@SUMMERSDALEBOOKS** and get in touch.
We'd love to hear from you!

WWW.SUMMERSDALE.COM

IMAGE CREDITS